But Noah **MISSED OUT** on fam
time and other fun things.

On Sunday, Dad and Liam asked Noah to go on a bike ride with them. But Noah wanted to watch TELEVISION.

4

I WANT TO WATCH!

LEARNING ABOUT SCREEN TIME

Katherine Eason

FOX EYE
PUBLISHING

Noah loved **SCREEN TIME**. He liked to watch a lot of TV. He liked playing video games. Sometimes, he played games on Mum's phone too.

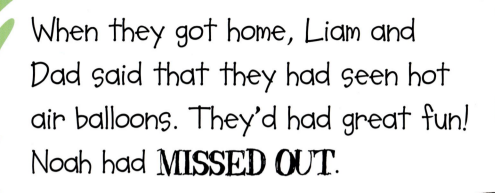

When they got home, Liam and Dad said that they had seen hot air balloons. They'd had great fun! Noah had **MISSED OUT**.

5

At lunchtime, Noah wanted to play with Mum's **PHONE**. The rule was no phones at the table. Noah played with the phone under the table.

Liam told a joke. Everyone laughed. But Noah didn't hear it. He **MISSED OUT!**

After lunch, Noah wanted to play a **VIDEO GAME**. But Mum said they were going to visit Granny and Grandpa. Noah sulked.

Grandpa made a swing with Liam in the garden. It was good fun! Noah **MISSED OUT**.

At bedtime, Noah sneaked downstairs and got his **GAME CONSOLE**. The rule was no video games before bed. When Dad came to say goodnight, Noah hid the console under his pillow.

Noah played on the game console after bedtime.

11

The next day, Noah's class had a spelling test. Noah was good at spelling. But he was **TOO TIRED** to remember his spellings.

Noah got all the spellings wrong.
He was **UPSET**.

Noah told Dad what had happened. Dad said too much screen time was bad for you. Rules about screen time were to keep you healthy and stop you from missing out. Dad asked Noah how he would feel if he missed all the fun?

After dinner, Noah played a board game
with Mum, Dad and Liam, and he won!
Liam told a joke, and everyone laughed.
They had a lot of fun.

16

Dad winked at Noah. Noah **FELT GOOD** because he **WASN'T MISSING OUT**.

Words and Behaviour

Noah had too much screen time in this story and that caused a lot of problems.

GAME CONSOLE

PHONE

SCREEN TIME

TELEVISION

There are a lot of words to do with screen time in this book. Can you remember all of them?

MISSED OUT

VIDEO GAME

Let's talk about feelings and manners

This series helps children to understand difficult emotions and behaviours and how to manage them. The characters in the series have been created to show emotions and behaviours that are often seen in young children, and which can be difficult to manage.

I Want to Watch!

The story in this book examines the reasons for controlling screen time. It looks at why controlling screen time is important and how it stops people from doing healthier activities such as enjoying family time.

How to use this book

You can read this book with one child or a group of children. The book can be used to begin a discussion around complex behaviour such as controlling screen time.

The book is also a reading aid, with enlarged and repeated words to help children to develop their reading skills.

How to read the story

Before beginning the story, ensure that the children you are reading to are relaxed and focused.

Take time to look at the enlarged words and the illustrations, and discuss what this book might be about before reading the story.

New words can be tricky for young children to approach. Sounding them out first, slowly and repeatedly, can help children to learn the words and become familiar with them.

How to discuss the story

When you have finished reading the story, use these questions and discussion points to examine the theme of the story with children and explore the emotions and behaviour within it:

- What do you think the story was about?
- Have you been in a situation in which you watched too much television/played too many video games? What was that situation?
- Do you think having too much television/video game time doesn't matter? Why?
- Do you think not having too much television/video game time is important? Why?
- What could go wrong if you have too much television/video game time?

Titles in the series

   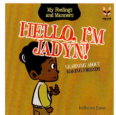 

 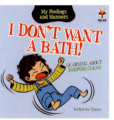   

 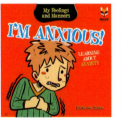  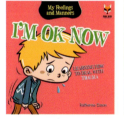 

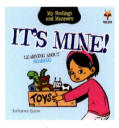    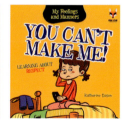

First published in 2023 by Fox Eye Publishing
Unit 31, Vulcan House Business Centre,
Vulcan Road, Leicester, LE5 3EF
www.foxeyepublishing.com

Author: Katherine Eason
Art director: Paul Phillips
Cover designer: Emma Bailey
Editor: Jenny Rush

All illustrations by Novel

ISBN 978-1-80445-165-6

Printed in China